# My Family Meal

## Working at the Same Time



Simone Braxt...

COMPUTER SCIENCE For the REAL World™

Rosen Classroom™

My family makes a meal.

We do different jobs
at the same time.
Dad and I chop peppers.

My mom and sister bake bread.
It smells yummy!

Dad and I make a salad.

We use many vegetables.

My mom and sister
cook noodles.
They put noodles in hot water.

The meal is done fast.

It's time to eat!

# Words to Know

bread

noodles

pepper

salad